FOREWORD

The collection of "Everything Will Be Okay" travel phrasebooks published by T&P Books is designed for people traveling abroad for tourism and business. The phrasebooks contain what matters most - the essentials for basic communication. This is an indispensable set of phrases to "survive" while abroad.

This phrasebook will help you in most cases where you need to ask something, get directions, find out how much something costs, etc. It can also resolve difficult communication situations where gestures just won't help.

This book contains a lot of phrases that have been grouped according to the most relevant topics. You'll also find a mini dictionary with useful words - numbers, time, calendar, colors...

Take "Everything Will Be Okay" phrasebook with you on the road and you'll have an irreplaceable traveling companion who will help you find your way out of any situation and teach you to not fear speaking with foreigners.

TABLE OF CONTENTS

T&P Books Publishing

Travel phrasebooks collection
«Everything Will Be Okay!»

T&P Books Publishing

PHRASEBOOK

- AFRIKAANS -

THE MOST IMPORTANT PHRASES

This phrasebook contains
the most important
phrases and questions
for basic communication
Everything you need
to survive overseas

By Andrey Taranov

T&P BOOKS

Phrasebook + 250-word dictionary

English-Afrikaans phrasebook & mini dictionary

By Andrey Taranov

The collection of "Everything Will Be Okay" travel phrasebooks published by T&P Books is designed for people traveling abroad for tourism and business. The phrasebooks contain what matters most - the essentials for basic communication. This is an indispensable set of phrases to "survive" while abroad.

You'll also find a mini dictionary with 250 useful words required for everyday communication - the names of months and days of the week, measurements, family members, and more.

T&P Books Publishing
www.tpbooks.com

ISBN: 978-1-78716-571-7

This book is also available in E-book formats.
Please visit www.tpbooks.com or the major online bookstores.

PRONUNCIATION

T&P phonetic alphabet	Afrikaans example	English example
[a]	land	shorter than in ask
[ã]	straat	calf, palm
[æ]	hout	chess, man
[ɔ], [ɔ]	Australië	drop, baught
[e]	metaal	elm, medal
[ɛ]	aanlê	man, bad
[ə]	filter	driver, teacher
[ɪ]	uur	big, America
[i]	billik	shorter than in feet
[ĩ]	naïef	tree, big
[o]	koppie	pod, John
[ø]	akteur	eternal, church
[œ]	fluit	German Hölle
[u]	hulle	book
[ʊ]	hout	good, booklet
[b]	bakker	baby, book
[d]	donder	day, doctor
[f]	navraag	face, food
[g]	burger	game, gold
[h]	driehoek	home, have
[j]	byvoeg	yes, New York
[k]	kamera	clock, kiss
[l]	loon	lace, people
[m]	môre	magic, milk
[n]	neef	sang, thing
[p]	pyp	pencil, private
[r]	rigting	rice, radio
[s]	oplos	city, boss
[t]	lood, tenk	tourist, trip
[v]	bewaar	very, river
[w]	oorwinnaar	vase, winter
[z]	zoem	zebra, please
[dʒ]	enjin	joke, general
[ʃ]	artisjok	machine, shark
[ŋ]	kans	English, ring

T&P phonetic alphabet	Afrikaans example	English example
[ʧ]	tjek	church, French
[ʒ]	beige	forge, pleasure
[x]	agent	as in Scots 'loch'

LIST OF ABBREVIATIONS

English abbreviations

ab.	-	about
adj	-	adjective
adv	-	adverb
anim.	-	animate
as adj	-	attributive noun used as adjective
e.g.	-	for example
etc.	-	et cetera
fam.	-	familiar
fem.	-	feminine
form.	-	formal
inanim.	-	inanimate
masc.	-	masculine
math	-	mathematics
mil.	-	military
n	-	noun
pl	-	plural
pron.	-	pronoun
sb	-	somebody
sing.	-	singular
sth	-	something
v aux	-	auxiliary verb
vi	-	intransitive verb
vi, vt	-	intransitive, transitive verb
vt	-	transitive verb

AFRIKAANS PHRASEBOOK

This section contains important phrases that may come in handy in various real-life situations.
The phrasebook will help you ask for directions, clarify a price, buy tickets, and order food at a restaurant

T&P Books Publishing

PHRASEBOOK CONTENTS

T&P Books Publishing

The bare minimum

Excuse me, ...	**Verskoon my, ...** [ferskoən maj, ...]
Hello.	**Hallo.** [hallo.]
Thank you.	**Baie dankie.** [baje danki.]
Good bye.	**Totsiens.** [totsiŋs.]
Yes.	**Ja.** [ja.]
No.	**Nee.** [neə.]
I don't know.	**Ek weet nie.** [ɛk veət ni.]
Where? | Where to? | When?	**Waar? | Waarheen? | Wanneer?** [vãr? | vãrheən? | vanneər?]

I need ...	**Ek het ... nodig** [ɛk het ... nodəχ]
I want ...	**Ek wil ...** [ɛk vil ...]
Do you have ...?	**Het u ...?** [het u ...?]
Is there a ... here?	**Is hier 'n ...?** [is hir ə ...?]
May I ...?	**Mag ek ...?** [maχ ek ...?]
..., please (polite request)	**... asseblief** [... asseblif]

I'm looking for ...	**Ek soek ...** [ɛk suk ...]
restroom	**toilet** [tojlet]
ATM	**OTM** [o·te·em]
pharmacy (drugstore)	**apteek** [apteək]
hospital	**hospitaal** [hospitãl]
police station	**polisiekantoor** [polisi·kantoər]
subway	**moltrein** [moltræjn]

taxi	**taxi** [taksi]
train station	**stasie** [stasi]

My name is ...	**My naam is ...** [maj nãm is ...]
What's your name?	**Wat is u naam?** [vat is u nãm?]
Could you please help me?	**Kan u my help, asseblief?** [kan u maj hɛlp, asseblif?]
I've got a problem.	**Ek het 'n probleem.** [ɛk het ə probleəm.]
I don't feel well.	**Ek voel nie lekker nie.** [ɛk ful ni lɛkkər ni.]
Call an ambulance!	**Bel 'n ambulans!** [bel ə ambulaŋs!]
May I make a call?	**Kan ek 'n oproep maak?** [kan ɛk ə oprup mãk?]

I'm sorry.	**Jammer.** [jammər.]
You're welcome.	**Plesier.** [plesir.]

I, me	**Ek, my** [ek, maj]
you (inform.)	**jy** [jaj]
he	**hy** [haj]
she	**sy** [saj]
they (masc.)	**hulle** [hullə]
they (fem.)	**hulle** [hullə]
we	**ons** [ɔŋs]
you (pl)	**julle** [jullə]
you (sg, form.)	**u** [u]

ENTRANCE	**INGANG** [inχaŋ]
EXIT	**UITGANG** [œitχaŋ]
OUT OF ORDER	**BUITE WERKING** [bœitə verkiŋ]
CLOSED	**GESLUIT** [χeslœit]

OPEN	**OOP** [oəp]
FOR WOMEN	**DAMES** [dames]
FOR MEN	**MANS** [maŋs]

Questions

Where?	**Waar?** [vãr?]
Where to?	**Waarheen?** [vãrheen?]
Where from?	**Van waar?** [fan vãr?]
Why?	**Waar?** [vãr?]
For what reason?	**Waarom?** [vãrom?]
When?	**Wanneer?** [vanneer?]
How long?	**Hoe lank?** [hu lank?]
At what time?	**Hoe laat?** [hu lãt?]
How much?	**Hoeveel?** [hufeel?]
Do you have ...?	**Het u ...?** [het u ...?]
Where is ...?	**Waar is ...?** [vãr is ...?]
What time is it?	**Hoe laat is dit?** [hu lãt is dit?]
May I make a call?	**Kan ek 'n oproep maak?** [kan ɛk ə oprup mãk?]
Who's there?	**Wie is daar?** [vi is dãr?]
Can I smoke here?	**Mag ek hier rook?** [maχ ek hir roek?]
May I ...?	**Mag ek ...?** [maχ ek ...?]

Needs

I'd like ...	**Ek sou graag ...** [ɛk sæʊ χrãχ ...]
I don't want ...	**Ek wil nie ...** [ɛk vil ni ...]
I'm thirsty.	**Ek is dors.** [ɛk is dors.]
I want to sleep.	**Ek wil slaap.** [ɛk vil slãp.]
I want ...	**Ek wil ...** [ɛk vil ...]
to wash up	**was** [vas]
to brush my teeth	**my tande borsel** [maj tandə borsəl]
to rest a while	**bietjie rus** [biki rus]
to change my clothes	**ander klere aantrek** [andər klerə ãntrek]
to go back to the hotel	**teruggaan hotel toe** [teruχχãn hotəl tu]
to buy ...	**... koop** [... koəp]
to go to ...	**gaan na ...** [χãn na ...]
to visit ...	**besoek ...** [besuk ...]
to meet with ...	**ontmoet ...** [ontmut ...]
to make a call	**bel** [bəl]
I'm tired.	**Ek is moeg.** [ɛk is muχ.]
We are tired.	**Ons is moeg.** [ɔŋs is muχ.]
I'm cold.	**Ek kry koud.** [ɛk kraj kæʊt.]
I'm hot.	**Ek kry warm.** [ɛk kraj varm.]
I'm OK.	**Ek is OK.** [ɛk is okej.]

I need to make a call. | **Ek moet 'n oproep maak.**
[ɛk mut ə oprup mãk.]

I need to go to the restroom. | **Ek moet toilet toe gaan.**
[ɛk mut toilet tu χãn.]

I have to go. | **Ek moet loop.**
[ɛk mut loəp.]

I have to go now. | **Ek moet nou loop.**
[ɛk mut næʊ loəp.]

Asking for directions

Excuse me, ...

Verskoon tog, ...
[ferskoən toχ, ...]

Where is ...?

Waar is ...?
[vãr is ...?]

Which way is ...?

In watter rigting is ...?
[in vattər riχtiŋ is ...?]

Could you help me, please?

Kan u my help, asseblief?
[kan u maj hɛlp, asseblif?]

I'm looking for ...

Ek soek ...
[ɛk suk ...]

I'm looking for the exit.

Waar is die uitgang?
[vãr is di œitχaŋ?]

I'm going to ...

Ek gaan na ...
[ɛk χãn na ...]

Am I going the right way to ...?

Is dit die regte pad na ...?
[is dit di reχtə pat na ...?]

Is it far?

Is dit ver?
[is dit fer?]

Can I get there on foot?

Kan ek te voet soontoe gaan?
[kan ɛk tə fut soentu χãn?]

Can you show me on the map?

Kan u dit op die kaart aanwys?
[kan u dit op di kãrt ãnwajs?]

Show me where we are right now.

Kan u my aanwys waar ons nou is?
[kan u maj ãnwajs vãr ɔŋs næʊ is?]

Here

Hier
[hir]

There

Daar
[dãr]

This way

Hiernatoe
[hirnatu]

Turn right.

Draai regs.
[drãj reχs.]

Turn left.

Draai links.
[drãj links.]

first (second, third) turn

eerste (tweede, derde) draai
[eərstə (tweədə, derdə) drãi]

to the right

na regs
[na reχs]

to the left

na links
[na links]

Go straight ahead.

Gaan reguit vorentoe.
[χān reχœit forentu.]

Signs

WELCOME!	**WELKOM!** [vɛlkom!]
ENTRANCE	**INGANG** [inχaŋ]
EXIT	**UITGANG** [œitχaŋ]
PUSH	**STOOT** [stoet]
PULL	**TREK** [trek]
OPEN	**OOP** [oəp]
CLOSED	**GESLUIT** [χeslœit]
FOR WOMEN	**DAMES** [dames]
FOR MEN	**MANS (M)** [maŋs]
GENTLEMEN, GENTS (m)	**MANS (M)** [maŋs]
WOMEN (f)	**DAMES (V)** [dames]
DISCOUNTS	**AFSLAG** [afslaχ]
SALE	**UITVERKOPING** [œitferkopiŋ]
FREE	**GRATIS** [χratis]
NEW!	**NUUT!** [nɪt!]
ATTENTION!	**PAS OP!** [pas op!]
NO VACANCIES	**KAMERS BESET** [kamers beset]
RESERVED	**BESPREEK** [bespreək]
ADMINISTRATION	**ADMINISTRASIE** [administrasi]
STAFF ONLY	**SLEGS PERSONEEL** [sleχs personeəl]

BEWARE OF THE DOG!	**PAS OP VIR DIE HOND** [pas op fir di hont]
NO SMOKING!	**ROOK VERBODE!** [roek ferbodə!]
DO NOT TOUCH!	**NIE AANRAAK NIE!** [ni ānrāk ni!]
DANGEROUS	**GEVAARLIK** [χefārlik]
DANGER	**GEVAAR** [χefār]
HIGH VOLTAGE	**HOOGSPANNING** [hoəχ·spaniŋ]
NO SWIMMING!	**SWEM VERBODE!** [swem ferbodə!]

OUT OF ORDER	**BUITE GEBRUIK** [bœitə χebrœik]
FLAMMABLE	**BRANDBAAR** [brantbār]
FORBIDDEN	**VERBODE** [ferbodə]
NO TRESPASSING!	**TOEGANG VERBODE!** [tuχaŋ ferbodə!]
WET PAINT	**NAT VERF** [nat ferf]

CLOSED FOR RENOVATIONS	**GESLUIT VIR HERSTELWERK** [χeslœit fir herstəl·werk]
WORKS AHEAD	**PADWERKE** [padwerkə]
DETOUR	**OMPAD** [ompat]

Transportation. General phrases

plane	**vliegtuig** [fliχtœix]
train	**trein** [træjn]
bus	**bus** [bus]
ferry	**veerboot** [feər·boət]
taxi	**taxi** [taksi]
car	**motor** [motor]
schedule	**diensrooster** [diŋs·roəstər]
Where can I see the schedule?	**Waar is die diensrooster?** [vãr is di diŋs·roəster?]
workdays (weekdays)	**werksdae** [verksdaə]
weekends	**naweke** [navekə]
holidays	**vakansies** [fakaŋsis]
DEPARTURE	**VERTREK** [fertrek]
ARRIVAL	**AANKOMS** [ãnkoms]
DELAYED	**VERTRAAG** [fertrãχ]
CANCELLED	**GEKANSELLEER** [χekaŋsɛlleər]
next (train, etc.)	**volgende** [folχendə]
first	**eerste** [eərstə]
last	**laaste** [lãstə]
When is the next ...?	**Wanneer vertrek die volgende ...?** [vanneər fertrek di folχendə ...?]
When is the first ...?	**Wanneer vertrek die eerste ...?** [vanneər fertrek di eərstə ...?]

When is the last ...?

Wanneer vertrek die laaste ...?
[vanneer fertrek di lāstə ...?]

transfer (change of trains, etc.)

aansluiting
[āŋslœitiŋ]

to make a transfer

oorstap
[oərstap]

Do I need to make a transfer?

Moet ek oorstap?
[mut ek oərstap?]

Buying tickets

Where can I buy tickets?	**Waar kan ek kaartjies koop?** [vãr kan ɛk kãrkis koəp?]
ticket	**kaartjie** [kãrki]
to buy a ticket	**'n kaartjie koop** [ə kãrki koəp]
ticket price	**kaartjie se prys** [kãrki sə prajs]
Where to?	**Waarheen?** [vãrheən?]
To what station?	**Na watter stasie?** [na vattər stasi?]
I need ...	**Ek het ... nodig** [ɛk het ... nodəχ]
one ticket	**'n kaartjie** [ə kãrki]
two tickets	**twee kaartjies** [tweə kãrkis]
three tickets	**drie kaartjies** [dri kãrkis]
one-way	**enkel** [ɛnkəl]
round-trip	**retoer** [retur]
first class	**eerste klas** [eərstə klas]
second class	**tweede klas** [tweədə klas]
today	**vandag** [fandaχ]
tomorrow	**môre** [mɔrə]
the day after tomorrow	**oormôre** [oərmɔrə]
in the morning	**soggens** [soχɛŋs]
in the afternoon	**smiddags** [smiddaχs]
in the evening	**saans** [sãŋs]

aisle seat	**sitplek langs die paadjie** [sitplek laŋs di pādʒi]
window seat	**venstersitplek** [fɛŋstər·sitplek]
How much?	**Hoeveel?** [hufeəl?]
Can I pay by credit card?	**Kan ek met 'n kredietkaart betaal?** [kan ɛk met ə kreditkārt betāl?]

Bus

bus	**bus** [bus]
intercity bus	**interstedelike bus** [interstedelikə bus]
bus stop	**bushalte** [bus·haltə]
Where's the nearest bus stop?	**Waar is die naaste bushalte?** [vār is di nāstə bus·halte?]
number (bus ~, etc.)	**nommer** [nommər]
Which bus do I take to get to …?	**Watter bus moet ek neem om na … te gaan?** [vattər bus mut ɛk neəm om na … tə χān?]
Does this bus go to …?	**Gaan hierdie bus na …?** [χān hirdi bus na …?]
How frequent are the buses?	**Hoe gereëld ry die busse?** [hu χerɛlt raj di bussə?]
every 15 minutes	**elke 15 minute** [ɛlkə fajftin minutə]
every half hour	**elke half uur** [ɛlkə half ɪr]
every hour	**elke uur** [ɛlkə ɪr]
several times a day	**verskillende kere per dag** [ferskillendə kerə pər daχ]
… times a day	**… kere per dag** [… kerə pər daχ]
schedule	**diensrooster** [diŋs·roəstər]
Where can I see the schedule?	**Waar is die diensrooster?** [vār is di diŋs·roəster?]
When is the next bus?	**Wanneer vertrek die volgende bus?** [vanneər fertrek di folχendə bus?]
When is the first bus?	**Wanneer vertrek die eerste bus?** [vanneər fertrek di eərstə bus?]
When is the last bus?	**Wanneer vertrek die laaste bus?** [vanneər fertrek di lāstə bus?]

stop	**halte** [haltə]
next stop	**volgende halte** [folχendə haltə]
last stop (terminus)	**eindpunt** [æjnd·punt]
Stop here, please.	**Stop hier, asseblief.** [stop hir, asseblif.]
Excuse me, this is my stop.	**Verskoon my, dis my halte.** [ferskoən maj, dis maj halte.]

Train

train	**trein** [træjn]
suburban train	**voorstedelike trein** [foərstedelikə træjn]
long-distance train	**langafstand trein** [lanχ·afstant træjn]
train station	**stasie** [stasi]
Excuse me, where is the exit to the platform?	**Verskoon my, waar is die uitgang na die perron?** [ferskoən maj, vār is di œitχaŋ na di perron?]

Does this train go to …?	**Gaan hierdie trein na …?** [χān hirdi træjn na …?]
next train	**volgende trein** [folχendə træjn]
When is the next train?	**Wanneer vertrek die volgende trein?** [vanneər fertrek di folχendə træjn?]
Where can I see the schedule?	**Waar is die diensrooster?** [vār is di diŋs·roəster?]
From which platform?	**Van watter perron?** [fan vattər perron?]
When does the train arrive in …?	**Wanneer kom die trein aan in …?** [vanneər kom di træjn ān in …?]

Please help me.	**Help my, asseblief.** [hɛlp maj, asseblif.]
I'm looking for my seat.	**Ek soek my sitplek.** [ɛk suk maj sitplek.]
We're looking for our seats.	**Ons soek ons sitplek.** [ɔŋs suk ɔŋs sitplek.]
My seat is taken.	**My sitplek is beset.** [maj sitplek is beset.]
Our seats are taken.	**Ons sitplekke is beset.** [ɔŋs sitplekkə is beset.]

I'm sorry but this is my seat.	**Jammer, dis my sitplek.** [jammər, dis maj sitplek.]
Is this seat taken?	**Is hierdie sitplek beset?** [is hirdi sitplek beset?]
May I sit here?	**Kan ek hier sit?** [kan ek hir sit?]

On the train. Dialogue (No ticket)

Ticket, please.	**Kaartjie, asseblief.** [kārki, asseblif.]
I don't have a ticket.	**Ek het nie 'n kaartjie nie.** [ɛk het ni ə kārki ni.]
I lost my ticket.	**Ek het my kaartjie verloor.** [ɛk het maj kārki ferloər.]
I forgot my ticket at home.	**Ek het my kaartjie by die huis vergeet.** [ɛk het maj kārki baj di hœis ferχeət.]

You can buy a ticket from me.	**U kan 'n kaartjie van my koop.** [u kan ə kārki fan maj koəp.]
You will also have to pay a fine.	**U moet 'n boete betaal.** [u mut ə butə betāl.]
Okay.	**Oukei.** [æʊkæj.]
Where are you going?	**Waarheen gaan u?** [vārheən χān u?]
I'm going to ...	**Ek gaan na ...** [ɛk χān na ...]

How much? I don't understand.	**Hoeveel kos dit? Ek verstaan dit nie.** [hufeəl kos dit? ek ferstān dit ni.]
Write it down, please.	**Skryf dit neer, asseblief.** [skrajf dit neər, asseblif.]
Okay. Can I pay with a credit card?	**OK. Kan ek met 'n kredietkaart betaal?** [okej. kan ɛk met ə kreditkārt betāl?]
Yes, you can.	**Ja, dit kan.** [ja, dit kan.]

Here's your receipt.	**Hier is u ontvangsbewys.** [hir is u ontfaŋs·bevajs.]
Sorry about the fine.	**Jammer vir die boete.** [jammer fir di bute.]
That's okay. It was my fault.	**Dis oukei. Dit was my skuld.** [dis æʊkæj. dit vas maj skult.]
Enjoy your trip.	**Geniet u reis.** [χenit u ræjs.]

Taxi

taxi	**taxi** [taksi]
taxi driver	**taxibestuurder** [taksi·bestɪrdər]
to catch a taxi	**'n taxi neem** [ə taksi neəm]
taxi stand	**taxistaanplek** [taksi·stānplek]
Where can I get a taxi?	**Waar kan ek 'n taxi neem?** [vār kan ɛk ə taksi neəm?]
to call a taxi	**'n taxi bel** [ə taksi bəl]
I need a taxi.	**Ek het 'n taxi nodig.** [ɛk het ə taksi nodəχ.]

Right now.	**Nou onmiddellik.** [næʊ onmiddɛllik.]
What is your address (location)?	**Wat is u adres?** [vat is u adres?]
My address is ...	**My adres is ...** [maj adres is ...]
Your destination?	**U bestemming?** [u bestɛmmiŋ?]
Excuse me, ...	**Verskoon tog, ...** [ferskoən toχ, ...]
Are you available?	**Is u vry?** [is u fraj?]
How much is it to get to ...?	**Hoeveel kos dit na ...?** [hufeəl kos dit na ...?]
Do you know where it is?	**Weet u waar dit is?** [veət u vār dit is?]

Airport, please.	**Lughawe, asseblief** [luχhavə, asseblif]
Stop here, please.	**Stop hier, asseblief.** [stop hir, asseblif.]
It's not here.	**Dis nie hier nie.** [dis ni hir ni.]
This is the wrong address.	**Dis die verkeerde adres.** [dis di ferkeərdə adres.]
Turn left.	**Draai links.** [drāj links.]
Turn right.	**Draai regs.** [drāj reχs.]

How much do I owe you?

Wat skuld ek u?
[vat skult ek u?]

I'd like a receipt, please.

Kan ek 'n ontvangsbewys kry, asseblief?
[kan ek ə ontfaŋs·bevajs kraj, asseblif?]

Keep the change.

Hou die kleingeld.
[hæʊ di klæjŋ·χɛlt.]

Would you please wait for me?

Sal u vir my wag, asseblief?
[sal u fir maj vaχ, asseblif?]

five minutes

vyf minute
[fajf minutə]

ten minutes

tien minute
[tin minutə]

fifteen minutes

vyftien minute
[fajftin minutə]

twenty minutes

twintig minute
[twintəχ minutə]

half an hour

'n halfuur
[ə halfɪr]

Hotel

Hello.	**Hallo.** [hallo.]
My name is ...	**My naam is ...** [maj nãm is ...]
I have a reservation.	**Ek het bespreek.** [ɛk het bespreek.]

I need ...	**Ek het ... nodig** [ɛk het ... nodəχ]
a single room	**'n enkelkamer** [ə ɛnkəl·kamər]
a double room	**'n dubbelkamer** [ə dubbəl·kamər]
How much is that?	**Hoeveel kos dit?** [hufeəl kos dit?]
That's a bit expensive.	**Dis nogal duur.** [dis noχal dɪr.]

Do you have anything else?	**Is daar nie ander moontlikhede nie?** [is dãr ni andər moentlikhedə ni?]
I'll take it.	**Ek vat dit.** [ɛk fat dit.]
I'll pay in cash.	**Ek betaal kontant.** [ɛk betãl kontant.]

I've got a problem.	**Ek het 'n probleem.** [ɛk het ə probleəm.]
My ... is broken.	**My ... is stukkend.** [maj ... is stukkent.]
My ... is out of order.	**My ... is buite werking.** [maj ... is bœeitə verkiŋ.]
TV	**TV** [te·fe]
air conditioner	**lugreëling** [luχreɛliŋ]
tap	**kraan** [krãn]

shower	**stortbad** [stortbat]
sink	**wasbak** [vasbak]
safe	**brandkas** [brant·kas]

door lock	**deur se slot** [døər sə slot]
electrical outlet	**stopkontak** [stop·kontak]
hairdryer	**haardroër** [hãr·droɛr]

I don't have …	**Ek het nie …** [ɛk het ni …]
water	**water** [vatər]
light	**lig** [liχ]
electricity	**krag** [kraχ]

Can you give me …?	**Kan u vir my … gee?** [kan u fir maj … χeə?]
a towel	**'n handdoek** [ə handduk]
a blanket	**'n kombers** [ə kombərs]
slippers	**pantoffels** [pantoffəls]
a robe	**'n kamerjas** [ə kamerjas]
shampoo	**sjampoe** [ʃampu]
soap	**seep** [seəp]

I'd like to change rooms.	**Ek wil van kamer verander.** [ɛk vil van kamər verandər.]
I can't find my key.	**Ek kan my sleutel nie vind nie.** [ɛk kan maj sløətəl ni fint ni.]
Could you open my room, please?	**Kan u my kamer oopsluit, asseblief?** [kan u maj kamər oəpslœit, asseblif?]
Who's there?	**Wie is daar?** [vi is dãr?]
Come in!	**Kom binne!** [kom binnə!]
Just a minute!	**'n Oomblik!** [ə oəmblik!]
Not right now, please.	**Nie nou nie, asseblief.** [ni næʊ ni, asseblif.]

Come to my room, please.	**Kom na my kamer, asseblief.** [kom na maj kamər, asseblif.]
I'd like to order food service.	**Kan ek kamerbediening kry.** [kan ɛk kamər·bediniŋ kraj.]
My room number is …	**My kamer se nommer is …** [maj kamər sə nommər is …]

I'm leaving ...	**Ek vertrek ...** [ɛk fertrək ...]
We're leaving ...	**Ons vertrek ...** [ɔŋs fertrek ...]
right now	**nou dadellik** [næʊ dadɛllik]
this afternoon	**vanmiddag** [fanmiddaχ]
tonight	**vanaand** [fanãnt]
tomorrow	**môre** [mɔrə]
tomorrow morning	**môreoggend** [mɔrə·oχent]
tomorrow evening	**môremiddag** [mɔrə·middaχ]
the day after tomorrow	**oormôre** [oərmɔrə]

I'd like to pay.	**Ek wil betaal.** [ɛk vil betãl.]
Everything was wonderful.	**Alles was uitstekend.** [alles vas œitstekent.]
Where can I get a taxi?	**Waar kan ek 'n taxi kry?** [vãr kan ɛk ə taksi kraj?]
Would you call a taxi for me, please?	**Sal u 'n taxi vir my bestel, asseblief.** [sal u ə taksi fir maj bestel, asseblif.]

Restaurant

Can I look at the menu, please?
Kan ek die spyskaart sien, asseblief?
[kan ɛk di spajskärt sin, asseblif?]

Table for one.
'n Tafel vir een persoon.
[ə tafəl fir eən persoən.]

There are two (three, four) of us.
Daar is twee (drie, vier) van ons.
[dār is tweə (dri, fir) fan ɔŋs.]

Smoking
Rook.
[roək.]

No smoking
Rook verbode.
[roək ferbodə.]

Excuse me! (addressing a waiter)
Hallo! Verskoning!
[hallo! ferskoniŋ!]

menu
spyskaart
[spajskärt]

wine list
wynkaart
[vajn·kärt]

The menu, please.
Die spyskaart, asseblief.
[di spajskärt, asseblif.]

Are you ready to order?
Is u gereed om te bestel?
[is u ɣereət om tə bestel?]

What will you have?
Wat verkies u?
[vat ferkis u?]

I'll have …
Ek wil … hê
[ɛk vil … hɛ:]

I'm a vegetarian.
Ek is vegetariër
[ɛk is feχetarier]

meat
vleis
[flæjs]

fish
vis
[fis]

vegetables
groente
[χruntə]

Do you have vegetarian dishes?
Het u vegetariese geregte?
[het u feχetarisə χereχtə?]

I don't eat pork.
Ek eet nie varkvleis nie.
[ɛk eət ni fark·flæjs ni.]

He /she/ doesn't eat meat.
Hy /sy/ eet nie vleis nie.
[haj /saj/ eət ni flæjs ni.]

I am allergic to …
Ek is allergies vir …
[ɛk is allerχis fir …]

Would you please bring me ...

Bring vir my ..., asseblief
[briŋ fir maj ..., asseblif]

salt | pepper | sugar

sout | peper | suiker
[sæʊt | pepər | sœikər]

coffee | tea | dessert

koffie | tee | nagereg
[koffi | teə | naχerəχ]

water | sparkling | plain

water | bruisend | plat
[vatər | brœisent | plat]

a spoon | fork | knife

'n lepel | vurk | mes
[ə lepəl | furk | mes]

a plate | napkin

'n bord | servet
[ə bort | serfet]

Enjoy your meal!

Smaaklike ete!
[smāklikə ete!]

One more, please.

Nog een, asseblief.
[noχ eən, asseblif.]

It was very delicious.

Dit was heerlik.
[dit vas heərlik.]

---

check | change | tip

rekening | wisselgeld | fooitjie
[rekəniŋ | vissəlχɛlt | fojki]

Check, please.
(Could I have the check, please?)

Die rekening, asseblief.
[di rekəniŋ, asseblif.]

Can I pay by credit card?

Kan ek met 'n kredietkaart betaal?
[kan ɛk met ə kreditkārt betāl?]

I'm sorry, there's a mistake here.

Jammer, hier is 'n fout.
[jammər, hir is ə fæʊt.]

Shopping

Can I help you?	**Kan ek help?** [kan ek hɛlp?]
Do you have ...?	**Het u ...?** [het u ...?]
I'm looking for ...	**Ek soek ...** [ɛk suk ...]
I need ...	**Ek het ... nodig** [ɛk het ... nodəx]
I'm just looking.	**Ek kyk net.** [ɛk kajk net.]
We're just looking.	**Ons kyk net.** [ɔŋs kajk net.]
I'll come back later.	**Ek kom netnou terug.** [ɛk kom netnæʊ teruχ.]
We'll come back later.	**Ons kom netnou terug.** [ɔŋs kom netnæʊ teruχ.]
discounts | sale	**afslag | uitverkoping** [afslaχ | œitferkopiŋ]
Would you please show me ...	**Kan u my ... wys, asseblief?** [kan u maj ... vajs, asseblif?]
Would you please give me ...	**Kan u my ... gee, asseblief?** [kan u maj ... χeə, asseblif?]
Can I try it on?	**Kan ek dit aanpas?** [kan ɛk dit ānpas?]
Excuse me, where's the fitting room?	**Verskoon tog, waar is die paskamer?** [ferskoən toχ, vār is di paskamer?]
Which color would you like?	**Watter kleur wil u hê?** [vattər kløər vil u hɛ:?]
size | length	**maat | lengte** [māt | leŋtə]
How does it fit?	**Pas dit?** [pas dit?]
How much is it?	**Hoeveel kos dit?** [hufeəl kos dit?]
That's too expensive.	**Dis te duur** [dis tə dɪr]
I'll take it.	**Ek sal dit vat.** [ɛk sal dit fat.]
Excuse me, where do I pay?	**Verskoon tog, waar moet ek betaal?** [ferskoən toχ, vār mut ek betāl?]

Will you pay in cash or credit card?	**Betaal u kontant of met 'n kredietkaart?** [betal u kontant of met ə kreditkãrt?]
In cash | with credit card	**kontant | met 'n kredietkaart** [kontant | met ə kreditkãrt]

Do you want the receipt?	**Wil u 'n ontvangsbewys?** [vil u ə ontfaŋsbevajs?]
Yes, please.	**Ja, asseblief.** [ja, asseblif.]
No, it's OK.	**Nee, dis nie nodig nie.** [neə, dis ni nodəχ ni.]
Thank you. Have a nice day!	**Dankie. Geniet die res van die dag!** [danki. χenit di res fan di daχ!]

In town

| Excuse me, please. | **Verskoon tog, asseblief.**
[ferskoən toχ, asseblif.] |
| I'm looking for ... | **Ek soek ...**
[ɛk suk ...] |

the subway	**die moltrein** [di moltræjn]
my hotel	**my hotel** [maj hotəl]
the movie theater	**die bioskoop** [di bioskoəp]
a taxi stand	**'n taxistaanplek** [ə taksi·stänplek]

an ATM	**'n OTM** [ə o·te·em]
a foreign exchange office	**'n wisselkantoor** [ə vissəl·kantoər]
an internet café	**'n internetkafee** [ə internet·kafeə]
... street	**... straat** [... strät]
this place	**hierdie plek** [hirdi plek]

| Do you know where ... is? | **Weet u waar ... is?**
[veət u vär ... is?] |
| Which street is this? | **Watter straat is dit?**
[vattər strät is dit?] |

Show me where we are right now.	**Kan u my aanwys waar ons nou is?** [kan u maj änwajs vär ɔŋs næʊ is?]
Can I get there on foot?	**Kan ek soontoe stap?** [kan ek soentu stap?]
Do you have a map of the city?	**Het u 'n kaart van die stad?** [het u ə kärt fan di stat?]

How much is a ticket to get in?	**Hoeveel kos 'n toegangskaartjie?** [hufeəl kos ə tuχaŋs·kärki?]
Can I take pictures here?	**Kan ek hier foto's maak?** [kan ɛk hir fotos mäk?]
Are you open?	**Is u oop?** [is u oəp?]

When do you open?

Hoe laat gaan u oop?
[hu lāt χān u oəp?]

When do you close?

Hoe laat sluit u?
[hu lāt slœit u?]

Money

money	**geld** [χɛlt]
cash	**kontant** [kontant]
paper money	**bankbiljette** [bank·biljɛttə]
loose change	**kleingeld** [klæjn·χɛlt]
check	change	tip	**rekening	wisselgeld	fooitjie** [rekəniŋ	vissəlχɛlt	fojki]
credit card	**kredietkaart** [kreditkãrt]
wallet	**beursie** [bøərsi]
to buy	**koop** [koəp]
to pay	**betaal** [betãl]
fine	**boete** [butə]
free	**gratis** [χratis]
Where can I buy …?	**Waar kan ek … koop?** [vãr kan ɛk … koəp?]
Is the bank open now?	**Is die bank nou oop?** [is di bank næʊ oəp?]
When does it open?	**Wanneer maak dit oop?** [vanneər mãk dit oəp?]
When does it close?	**Wanneer maak dit toe?** [vanneər mãk dit tu?]
How much?	**Hoeveel?** [hufeəl?]
How much is this?	**Hoeveel kos dit?** [hufeəl kos dit?]
That's too expensive.	**Dis te duur.** [dis tə dɪr.]
Excuse me, where do I pay?	**Verskoon tog, waar moet ek betaal?** [ferskoən toχ, vãr mut ek betãl?]
Check, please.	**Die rekening, asseblief.** [di rekəniŋ, asseblif.]

Can I pay by credit card?

Kan ek met 'n kredietkaart betaal?
[kan ɛk met ə kreditkãrt betãl?]

Is there an ATM here?

Verskoon tog, is hier 'n OTM?
[ferskoən toχ, is hir ə o·te·em?]

I'm looking for an ATM.

Ek soek 'n OTM.
[ɛk suk ə o·te·em.]

I'm looking for a foreign exchange office.

Ek soek 'n wisselkantoor.
[ɛk suk ə vissəl·kantoər.]

I'd like to change ...

Ek sou ... wou wissel.
[ɛk sæʊ ... væʊ vissəl.]

What is the exchange rate?

Wat is die wisselkoers?
[vat is di vissəlkurs?]

Do you need my passport?

Het u my paspoort nodig?
[het u maj paspoərt nodəχ?]

Time

What time is it?	**Hoe laat is dit?** [hu lãt is dit?]
When?	**Wanneer?** [vanneər?]
At what time?	**Hoe laat?** [hu lãt?]
now | later | after ...	**nou | later | na ...** [næʊ | latər | na ...]
one o'clock	**een uur** [eən ɪr]
one fifteen	**kwart oor een** [kwart oər eən]
one thirty	**half twee** [half tweə]
one forty-five	**kwart voor twee** [kwart foər tweə]
one | two | three	**een | twee | drie** [eən | tweə | dri]
four | five | six	**vier | vyf | ses** [fir | fajf | ses]
seven | eight | nine	**sewe | ag | nege** [sevə | aχ | neχə]
ten | eleven | twelve	**tien | elf | twaalf** [tin | ɛlf | twãlf]
in ...	**binne ...** [binnə ...]
five minutes	**vyf minute** [fajf minutə]
ten minutes	**tien minute** [tin minutə]
fifteen minutes	**vyftien minute** [fajftin minutə]
twenty minutes	**twintig minute** [twintəχ minutə]
half an hour	**'n halfuur** [ə halfɪr]
an hour	**'n uur** [ə ɪr]

in the morning	**soggens** [soχɛŋs]
early in the morning	**soggens vroeg** [soχɛŋs fruχ]
this morning	**vanoggend** [fanoχent]
tomorrow morning	**môreoggend** [mɔrə·oχent]

in the middle of the day	**in die middel van die dag** [in di middəl fan di daχ]
in the afternoon	**smiddags** [smiddaχs]
in the evening	**saans** [sāŋs]
tonight	**vanaand** [fanānt]

at night	**saans** [sāŋs]
yesterday	**gister** [χistər]
today	**vandag** [fandaχ]
tomorrow	**môre** [mɔrə]
the day after tomorrow	**oormôre** [oərmɔrə]

What day is it today?	**Watter dag is dit vandag?** [vattər daχ is dit fandaχ?]
It's ...	**Dit is ...** [dit is ...]
Monday	**maandag** [mãndaχ]
Tuesday	**dinsdag** [dinsdaχ]
Wednesday	**woensdag** [voɛŋsdaχ]

Thursday	**Donderdag** [dondərdaχ]
Friday	**vrydag** [frajdaχ]
Saturday	**saterdag** [satərdaχ]
Sunday	**sondag** [sondaχ]

Greetings. Introductions

Hello.
Hallo.
[hallo.]

Pleased to meet you.
Aangename kennis.
[ānχənamə kɛnnis.]

Me too.
Dieselfde.
[disɛlfdə.]

I'd like you to meet ...
Kan ek jou voorstel aan ...
[kan ɛk jæʊ foərstəl ān ...]

Nice to meet you.
Aangename kennis.
[ānχənamə kɛnnis.]

How are you?
Hoe gaan dit?
[hu χān dit?]

My name is ...
My naam is ...
[maj nām is ...]

His name is ...
Dis ...
[dis ...]

Her name is ...
Dis ...
[dis ...]

What's your name?
Wat is u naam?
[vat is u nām?]

What's his name?
Wat is sy naam?
[vat is saj nām?]

What's her name?
Wat is haar naam?
[vat is hār nām?]

What's your last name?
Wat is u van?
[vat is u fan?]

You can call me ...
Noem my maar ...
[num maj mār ...]

Where are you from?
Vanwaar kom u?
[fanwār kom u?]

I'm from ...
Ek kom van ...
[ɛk kom fan ...]

What do you do for a living?
Wat is u beroep?
[vat is u bərup?]

Who is this?
Wie is dit?
[vi is dit?]

Who is he?
Wie is hy?
[vi is haj?]

Who is she?
Wie is sy?
[vi is saj?]

Who are they?
Wie is hulle?
[vi is hullə?]

This is ...	**Dit is ...** [dit is ...]
my friend (masc.)	**my vriend** [maj frint]
my friend (fem.)	**my vriendin** [maj frindin]
my husband	**my man** [maj man]
my wife	**my vrou** [maj fræʊ]

my father	**my vader** [maj fadər]
my mother	**my moeder** [maj mudər]
my brother	**my broer** [maj brur]
my son	**my seun** [maj søən]
my daughter	**my dogter** [maj doχtər]

This is our son.	**Dit is ons seun.** [dit is ɔŋs søən.]
This is our daughter.	**Dit is ons dogter.** [dit is ɔŋs doχter.]
These are my children.	**Dit is my kinders.** [dit is maj kindərs.]
These are our children.	**Dit is ons kinders.** [dit is ɔŋs kindərs.]

Farewells

Good bye!	**Totsiens!** [totsiŋs!]
Bye! (inform.)	**Koebaai!** [kubāi!]
See you tomorrow.	**Sien jou môre.** [sin jæʊ mɔrə.]
See you soon.	**Totsiens.** [totsiŋs.]
See you at seven.	**Sien jou om sewe uur.** [sin jæʊ om sevə ɪr.]
Have fun!	**Geniet dit!** [χenit dit!]
Talk to you later.	**Gesels later.** [χesɛls latər.]
Have a nice weekend.	**Geniet die naweek.** [χenit di naveǝk.]
Good night.	**Lekker slaap.** [lɛkkər slāp.]
It's time for me to go.	**Dis tyd om te gaan.** [dis tajt om tǝ χān.]
I have to go.	**Ek moet loop.** [ɛk mut loǝp.]
I will be right back.	**Ek is nounou terug.** [ɛk is næʊnæʊ teruχ.]
It's late.	**Dis al laat.** [dis al lāt.]
I have to get up early.	**Ek moet vroeg opstaan.** [ɛk mut fruχ opstān.]
I'm leaving tomorrow.	**Ek vertrek môre.** [ɛk fertrǝk mɔrə.]
We're leaving tomorrow.	**Ons vertrek môre.** [ɔŋs fertrek mɔrə.]
Have a nice trip!	**Geniet die reis!** [χenit di ræjs!]
It was nice meeting you.	**Ek het dit geniet om jou te ontmoet.** [ɛk het dit χenit om jæʊ tǝ ontmut.]
It was nice talking to you.	**Dit was lekker om met jou te gesels.** [dit vas lɛkkǝr om met jæʊ tǝ χesɛls.]
Thanks for everything.	**Baie dankie vir alles.** [baje danki fir alles.]

I had a very good time.

Ek het dit geniet.
[ɛk het dit χenit.]

We had a very good time.

Ons het dit baie geniet.
[ɔŋs het dit baje χenit.]

It was really great.

Dit was regtig oulik.
[dit vas reχtəχ æʊlik.]

I'm going to miss you.

Ek gaan jou mis.
[ɛk χān jæʊ mis.]

We're going to miss you.

Ons gaan jou mis.
[ɔŋs χān jæʊ mis.]

Good luck!

Sukses!
[suksɛs!]

Say hi to ...

Stuur groete vir ...
[stɪr χrutə fir ...]

Foreign language

I don't understand.	**Ek verstaan dit nie.** [ɛk ferstãn dit ni.]
Write it down, please.	**Skryf dit neer, asseblief.** [skrajf dit neər, asseblif.]
Do you speak ...?	**Praat u ...?** [prãt u ...?]

I speak a little bit of ...	**Ek praat 'n bietjie ...** [ɛk prãt ə biki ...]
English	**Engels** [ɛŋəls]
Turkish	**Turks** [turks]
Arabic	**Arabies** [arabis]
French	**Frans** [fraŋs]

German	**Duits** [dœits]
Italian	**Italiaans** [italiãŋs]
Spanish	**Spaans** [spãŋs]
Portuguese	**Portugees** [portuχeəs]
Chinese	**Sjinees** [ʃineəs]
Japanese	**Japannees** [japanneəs]

Can you repeat that, please.	**Kan u dit herhaal asseblief** [kan u dit herhãl asseblif]
I understand.	**Ek verstaan dit.** [ɛk ferstãn dit.]
I don't understand.	**Ek verstaan dit nie.** [ɛk ferstãn dit ni.]
Please speak more slowly.	**Praat bietjie stadiger asseblief.** [prãt biki stadiχər asseblif.]

Is that correct? (Am I saying it right?)	**Is dit reg?** [is dit reχ?]
What is this? (What does this mean?)	**Wat is dit?** [vat is dit?]

Apologies

Excuse me, please.	**Verskoon my, asseblief.** [ferskoən maj, asseblif.]
I'm sorry.	**Jammer.** [jammər.]
I'm really sorry.	**Ek is baie jammer.** [ɛk is baje jammər.]
Sorry, it's my fault.	**Jammer, dis my skuld.** [jammər, dis maj skult.]
My mistake.	**My skuld.** [maj skult.]

May I ...?	**Mag ek ...?** [maχ ek ...?]
Do you mind if I ...?	**Sal u omgee as ek ...?** [sal u omχeə as ek ...?]
It's OK.	**Dis OK.** [dis okej.]
It's all right.	**Maak nie saak nie.** [māk ni sāk ni.]
Don't worry about it.	**Moet jou nie daaroor bekommer nie.** [mut jæʊ ni dāroər bekommər ni.]

Agreement

Yes.	**Ja.** [ja.]
Yes, sure.	**Ja, beslis.** [ja, beslis.]
OK (Good!)	**OK. Goed!** [okej. χut!]
Very well.	**Uitstekend.** [œitstekent]
Certainly!	**Definitief!** [definitif!]
I agree.	**Ek stem saam.** [ɛk stem sãm.]
That's correct.	**Dis reg.** [dis reχ.]
That's right.	**Dis reg.** [dis reχ.]
You're right.	**U is reg.** [u is reχ.]
I don't mind.	**Ek gee nie om nie.** [ɛk χeə ni om ni.]
Absolutely right.	**Heeltemal reg.** [heəltemal reχ.]
It's possible.	**Dis moontlik.** [dis moentlik.]
That's a good idea.	**Dis 'n goeie idee.** [dis ə χuje ideə.]
I can't say no.	**Ek kan nie nee sê nie.** [ɛk kan ni neə sɛ: ni.]
I'd be happy to.	**Dis 'n plesier.** [dis ə plesir.]
With pleasure.	**Plesier.** [plesir.]

Refusal. Expressing doubt

No.	**Nee** [neə]
Certainly not.	**Beslis nie.** [beslis ni.]
I don't agree.	**Ek stem nie saam nie.** [ɛk stem ni sãm ni.]
I don't think so.	**Ek glo dit nie.** [ɛk χlo dit ni.]
It's not true.	**Dis nie waar nie.** [dis ni vãr ni.]
You are wrong.	**U maak 'n fout.** [u mãk ə fæʊt.]
I think you are wrong.	**Ek dink u is verkeerd.** [ɛk dink u is ferkeərt.]
I'm not sure.	**Ek is nie seker nie.** [ɛk is ni sekər ni.]
It's impossible.	**Dis onmoontlik.** [dis onmoentlik.]
Nothing of the kind (sort)!	**Glad nie!** [χlat ni!]
The exact opposite.	**Net die teenoorgestelde!** [net di teənoərχestɛlde!]
I'm against it.	**Ek is daarteen.** [ɛk is dãrteən.]
I don't care.	**Ek gee nie om nie.** [ɛk χeə ni om ni.]
I have no idea.	**Ek het nie 'n idee nie.** [ɛk het ni ə ideə ni.]
I doubt it.	**Ek betwyfel dit.** [ɛk betwajfəl dit.]
Sorry, I can't.	**Jammer, ek kan nie.** [jammər, ɛk kan ni.]
Sorry, I don't want to.	**Jammer, ek wil nie.** [jammər, ɛk vil ni.]
Thank you, but I don't need this.	**Dankie, maar ek het dit nie nodig nie.** [danki, mãr ɛk het dit ni nodəχ ni.]
It's getting late.	**Dit word laat.** [dit vort lãt.]

I have to get up early.

Ek moet vroeg opstaan.
[ɛk mut fruχ opstãn.]

I don't feel well.

Ek voel nie lekker nie.
[ɛk ful ni lɛkkər ni.]

Expressing gratitude

Thank you.	**Baie dankie.** [baje danki.]
Thank you very much.	**Baie dankie.** [baje danki.]
I really appreciate it.	**Ek waardeer dit.** [ɛk vǎrdeǝr dit.]
I'm really grateful to you.	**Ek is u baie dankbaar.** [ɛk is u baje dankbǎr.]
We are really grateful to you.	**Ons is u baie dankbaar.** [ɔŋs is u baje dankbǎr.]
Thank you for your time.	**Baie dankie vir u tyd.** [baje danki fir u tajt.]
Thanks for everything.	**Baie dankie vir alles.** [baje danki fir alles.]
Thank you for ...	**Dankie vir ...** [danki fir ...]
your help	**u hulp** [u hulp]
a nice time	**vir 'n lekker tydjie** [fir ǝ lɛkkǝr tajdʒi]
a wonderful meal	**'n heerlike ete** [ǝ heǝrlikǝ etǝ]
a pleasant evening	**'n aangename aand** [ǝ ǎnχǝnamǝ ǎnt]
a wonderful day	**'n oulike dag** [ǝ æʊlikǝ daχ]
an amazing journey	**'n wonderlike reis** [ǝ vondǝrlikǝ ræjs]
Don't mention it.	**Plesier.** [plesir.]
You are welcome.	**Plesier.** [plesir.]
Any time.	**Enige tyd.** [ɛniχǝ tajt.]
My pleasure.	**Plesier.** [plesir.]
Forget it.	**Plesier.** [plesir.]
Don't worry about it.	**Moet jou nie bekommer nie.** [mut jæʊ ni bekommǝr ni.]

Congratulations. Best wishes

Congratulations!
Geluk!
[χeluk!]

Happy birthday!
Geluk met jou verjaardag!
[χeluk met jæʊ ferjȃrdaχ!]

Merry Christmas!
Geseënde Kersfees!
[χeseɛndə kersfeɛs!]

Happy New Year!
Gelukkige Nuwejaar!
[χelukkiχə nuvejȃr!]

Happy Easter!
Geseënde Paasfees!
[χeseɛndə pȃsfeɛs!]

Happy Hanukkah!
Gelukkige Chanoeka!
[χelukkiχə χanuka!]

I'd like to propose a toast.
Ek wil graag 'n heildronk instel.
[ɛk vil χrȃχ ə hæjldronk instəl.]

Cheers!
Gesondheid!
[χesonthæjt!]

Let's drink to ...!
Laat ons drink op ...!
[lȃt ɔŋs drink op ...!]

To our success!
Op jou sukses!
[op jæʊ suksɛs!]

To your success!
Op u sukses!
[op u suksɛs!]

Good luck!
Sukses!
[suksɛs!]

Have a nice day!
Geniet die dag!
[χenit di daχ!]

Have a good holiday!
Geniet die vakansie!
[χenit di fakaŋsi!]

Have a safe journey!
Veilig ry!
[fæjləχ raj!]

I hope you get better soon!
Ek hoop u voel gou beter!
[ɛk hoəp u ful χæʊ betər!]

Socializing

Why are you sad?	**Hoekom lyk u so droewig?** [hukom lajk u so druvəχ?]
Smile! Cheer up!	**Lag 'n bietjie! Wees vrolik!** [laχ ə biki! veəs frolik!]
Are you free tonight?	**Is u vry vanaand?** [is u fraj fanãnt?]
May I offer you a drink?	**Kan ek 'n drankie vir jou kry?** [kan ek ə dranki fir jæʊ kraj?]
Would you like to dance?	**Wil u dans?** [vil u daŋs?]
Let's go to the movies.	**Sal ons bioskoop toe gaan?** [sal ɔŋs bioskoəp tu χãn?]
May I invite you to …?	**Mag ek jou uitnooi na …?** [maχ ek jæʊ œitnoj na …?]
a restaurant	**'n restaurant** [ə restɔurant]
the movies	**die bioskoop** [di bioskoəp]
the theater	**die teater** [di teatər]
go for a walk	**gaan stap** [χãn stap]
At what time?	**Hoe laat?** [hu lãt?]
tonight	**vanaand** [fanãnt]
at six	**om ses uur** [om ses ɪr]
at seven	**om sewe uur** [om sevə ɪr]
at eight	**om agt uur** [om aχt ɪr]
at nine	**om nege uur** [om neχə ɪr]
Do you like it here?	**Geniet u dit hier?** [χenit u dit hir?]
Are you here with someone?	**Is u hier saam met iemand?** [is u hir sãm met imant?]
I'm with my friend.	**Ek is met my vriend.** [ɛk is met maj frint.]

I'm with my friends.	**Ek is met my vriende.** [ɛk is met maj frində.]
No, I'm alone.	**Nee, ek is alleen.** [neə, ek is alleən.]

Do you have a boyfriend?	**Het jy 'n kêrel?** [het jaj ə kærel?]
I have a boyfriend.	**Ek het 'n kêrel.** [ɛk het ə kærel.]
Do you have a girlfriend?	**Het jy 'n meisie?** [het jaj ə mæjsi?]
I have a girlfriend.	**Ek het 'n meisie.** [ɛk het ə mæjsi.]

Can I see you again?	**Kan ek jou weer sien?** [kan ek jæʊ veər sin?]
Can I call you?	**Kan ek jou bel?** [kan ek jæʊ bel?]
Call me. (Give me a call.)	**Bel my.** [bel maj.]
What's your number?	**Wat is jou nommer?** [vat is jæʊ nommər?]
I miss you.	**Ek mis jou.** [ɛk mis jæʊ.]

You have a beautiful name.	**U het 'n mooi naam.** [u het ə moj nãm.]
I love you.	**Ek hou van jou.** [ɛk hæʊ fan jæʊ.]
Will you marry me?	**Wil jy met my trou?** [vil jaj met maj træʊ?]
You're kidding!	**U maak grappies!** [u mãk χrappis!]
I'm just kidding.	**Ek maak net 'n grappie.** [ɛk mãk net ə χrappi.]

Are you serious?	**Bedoel u dit?** [bedul u dit?]
I'm serious.	**Ek is ernstig.** [ɛk is ernsteχ.]
Really?!	**Regtig waar?!** [reχteχ vãr?!]
It's unbelievable!	**Dis ongelooflik.** [dis onχeloəflik.]
I don't believe you.	**Ek glo jou nie.** [ɛk χlo jæʊ ni.]
I can't.	**Ek kan nie.** [ɛk kan ni.]
I don't know.	**Ek weet dit nie.** [ɛk veət dit ni.]
I don't understand you.	**Ek verstaan u nie.** [ɛk ferstãn u ni.]

Please go away.

Loop asseblief.
[loəp asseblif.]

Leave me alone!

Los my uit!
[los maj œit!]

I can't stand him.

Ek kan hom nie verdra nie.
[ɛk kan hom ni ferdra ni.]

You are disgusting!

U is walglik!
[u is valχlik!]

I'll call the police!

Ek gaan die polisie bel!
[ɛk χān di polisi bel!]

Sharing impressions. Emotions

I like it.	**Ek hou daarvan.** [ɛk hæʊ dãrfan.]
Very nice.	**Baie mooi.** [baje moj.]
That's great!	**Dis oulik!** [dis æʊlik!]
It's not bad.	**Dis nie sleg nie.** [dis ni sleχ ni.]

I don't like it.	**Ek hou nie daarvan nie.** [ɛk hæʊ ni dãrfan ni.]
It's not good.	**Dis nie goed nie.** [dis ni χut ni.]
It's bad.	**Dis sleg.** [dis sleχ.]
It's very bad.	**Dis baie sleg.** [dis baje sleχ.]
It's disgusting.	**Dis walglik.** [dis valχlik.]

I'm happy.	**Ek is bly.** [ɛk is blaj.]
I'm content.	**Ek is tevrede.** [ɛk is tefrede.]
I'm in love.	**Ek is verlief.** [ɛk is ferlif.]
I'm calm.	**Ek is rustig.** [ɛk is rusteχ.]
I'm bored.	**Ek verveel my.** [ɛk ferfeəl maj.]

I'm tired.	**Ek is moeg.** [ɛk is muχ.]
I'm sad.	**Ek is droewig.** [ɛk is druveχ.]
I'm frightened.	**Ek is bang.** [ɛk is baŋ.]

I'm angry.	**Ek is kwaad.** [ɛk is kwãt.]
I'm worried.	**Ek is bekommerd.** [ɛk is bekommert.]
I'm nervous.	**Ek is senuweeagtig.** [ɛk is senuveə aχteχ.]

I'm jealous. (envious)	**Ek is jaloers.** [ɛk is jalurs.]
I'm surprised.	**Dit verbaas my.** [dit ferbãs maj.]
I'm perplexed.	**Ek is verbouereerd.** [ɛk is ferbæʊreərt.]

Problems. Accidents

I've got a problem.	**Ek het 'n probleem.** [ɛk het ə probleəm.]
We've got a problem.	**Ons het 'n probleem.** [ɔŋs het ə probleəm.]
I'm lost.	**Ek het verdwaal.** [ɛk het ferdwāl.]
I missed the last bus (train).	**Ek het die laaste bus (trein) gemis.** [ɛk het di lāstə bus (træjn) χemis.]
I don't have any money left.	**My geld is op.** [maj χɛlt is op.]

I've lost my ...	**Ek het my ... verloor** [ɛk het maj ... ferloər]
Someone stole my ...	**Lemand het my ... gesteel.** [lemant het maj ... χesteəl.]
passport	**paspoort** [paspoərt]
wallet	**beursie** [bøərsi]
papers	**papiere** [papirə]
ticket	**kaartjie** [kārki]

money	**geld** [χɛlt]
handbag	**handsak** [hand·sak]
camera	**kamera** [kamera]
laptop	**skootrekenaar** [skoət·rekənār]
tablet computer	**tablet** [tablet]
mobile phone	**selfoon** [sɛlfoən]

Help me!	**Help!** [hɛlp!]
What's happened?	**Wat's fout?** [vats fæʊt?]
fire	**brand** [brant]

shooting	**daar word geskiet** [dãr vort χeskit]
murder	**moord** [moərt]
explosion	**ontploffing** [ontploffiŋ]
fight	**geveg** [χefeχ]

Call the police!	**Bel die polisie!** [bel di polisi!]
Please hurry up!	**Maak gou asseblief!** [mãk χæʊ asseblif!]
I'm looking for the police station.	**Ek soek die polisiekantoor.** [ɛk suk di polisi·kantoər.]
I need to make a call.	**Ek moet bel.** [ɛk mut bel.]
May I use your phone?	**Mag ek u telefoon gebruik?** [maχ ek u telefoən χebrœik?]

I've been ...	**Ek is ...** [ɛk is ...]
mugged	**aangeval** [ãnχəfal]
robbed	**beroof** [beroəf]
raped	**verkrag** [ferkraχ]
attacked (beaten up)	**aangeval** [ãnχəfal]

Are you all right?	**Gaan dit?** [χãn dit?]
Did you see who it was?	**Het u gesien wie dit was?** [het u χesin vi dit vas?]
Would you be able to recognize the person?	**Sou u die persoon kon herken?** [sæʊ u di persoən kon herken?]
Are you sure?	**Is u seker?** [is u seker?]

Please calm down.	**Kom tot bedaring asseblief.** [kom tot bedariŋ asseblif.]
Take it easy!	**Rustig!** [rustəχ!]
Don't worry!	**Moenie bekommerd wees nie!** [muni bekommert veəs ni!]
Everything will be fine.	**Alles sal reg kom.** [alles sal reχ kom.]
Everything's all right.	**Alles is reg.** [alles is reχ.]
Come here, please.	**Kom hier asseblief.** [kom hir asseblif.]

I have some questions for you.

Ek het 'n paar vrae vir u.
[ɛk het ə pãr fraə fir u.]

Wait a moment, please.

Wag 'n bietjie, asseblief.
[vaχ ə biki, asseblif.]

Do you have any I.D.?

Het u 'n identiteitskaart?
[het u ə identitæjts·kãrt?]

Thanks. You can leave now.

Dankie. U kan nou loop.
[danki. u kan næʊ loəp.]

Hands behind your head!

Hande agter jou kop!
[handə aχtər jæʊ kop!]

You're under arrest!

U is onder arres!
[u is ondər arres!]

Health problems

Please help me.	**Help my, asseblief.** [hɛlp maj, asseblif.]
I don't feel well.	**Ek voel nie lekker nie.** [ɛk ful ni lɛkkər ni.]
My husband doesn't feel well.	**My man voel nie lekker nie.** [maj man ful ni lɛkkər ni.]
My son ...	**My seun ...** [maj søən ...]
My father ...	**My pa ...** [maj pa ...]
My wife doesn't feel well.	**My vrou voel nie lekker nie.** [maj fræʊ ful ni lɛkkər ni.]
My daughter ...	**My dogter ...** [maj doχtər ...]
My mother ...	**My ma ...** [maj ma ...]
I've got a ...	**Ek het ...** [ɛk het ...]
headache	**koppyn** [koppajn]
sore throat	**keelpyn** [keəl·pajn]
stomach ache	**maagpyn** [māχpajn]
toothache	**tandpyn** [tand·pajn]
I feel dizzy.	**Ek voel duiselig.** [ɛk ful dœiselǝχ.]
He has a fever.	**Hy het koors.** [haj het koərs.]
She has a fever.	**Sy het koors.** [saj het koərs.]
I can't breathe.	**Ek kan nie goed asemhaal nie.** [ɛk kan ni χut asemhāl ni.]
I'm short of breath.	**Ek is kortasem.** [ɛk is kortasem.]
I am asthmatic.	**Ek is asmaties.** [ɛk is asmatis.]
I am diabetic.	**Ek is diabeet.** [ɛk is diabeət.]

I can't sleep.	**Ek kan nie slaap nie.** [ɛk kan ni slāp ni.]
food poisoning	**voedselvergiftiging** [fudsəl·ferχiftəχiŋ]

It hurts here.	**Dis seer hier.** [dis seǝr hir.]
Help me!	**Help!** [hɛlp!]
I am here!	**Ek is hier!** [ɛk is hir!]
We are here!	**Ons is hier!** [oŋs is hir!]
Get me out of here!	**Kom kry my!** [kom kraj maj!]
I need a doctor.	**Ek het 'n dokter nodig.** [ɛk het ǝ doktǝr nodǝχ.]
I can't move.	**Ek kan nie beweeg nie.** [ɛk kan ni beveǝχ ni.]
I can't move my legs.	**Ek kan my bene nie beweeg nie.** [ɛk kan maj benǝ ni beveǝχ ni.]

I have a wound.	**Ek het 'n wond.** [ɛk het ǝ vont.]
Is it serious?	**Is dit ernstig?** [is dit ernstǝχ?]
My documents are in my pocket.	**My dokumente is in my sak.** [maj dokumentǝ is in maj sak.]
Calm down!	**Bedaar!** [bedār!]
May I use your phone?	**Mag ek u telefoon gebruik?** [maχ ek u telefoǝn χebrœik?]

Call an ambulance!	**Bel 'n ambulans!** [bel ǝ ambulaŋs!]
It's urgent!	**Dis dringend!** [dis driŋǝnd!]
It's an emergency!	**Dis 'n noodgeval!** [dis ǝ noǝdχefal!]
Please hurry up!	**Maak gou asseblief!** [māk χæʊ asseblif!]
Would you please call a doctor?	**Kan u asseblief 'n dokter bel?** [kan u asseblif ǝ doktǝr bel?]
Where is the hospital?	**Waar is die hospitaal?** [vār is di hospitāl?]

How are you feeling?	**Hoe voel u?** [hu ful u?]
Are you all right?	**Hoe gaan dit?** [hu χān dit?]
What's happened?	**Wat het gebeur?** [vat het χebøǝr?]

I feel better now.

Ek voel nou beter.
[ɛk ful næu betər.]

It's OK.

Dis OK.
[dis okej.]

It's all right.

Dit gaan goed.
[dit χãn χut.]

At the pharmacy

pharmacy (drugstore)	**apteek** [apteək]
24-hour pharmacy	**24 uur apteek** [fir-en-twintəχ ɪr apteək]
Where is the closest pharmacy?	**Waar is die naaste apteek?** [vãr is di nãstə apteək?]
Is it open now?	**Is hy nou oop?** [is haj næʊ oəp?]
At what time does it open?	**Hoe laat gaan hy oop?** [hu lãt χãn haj oəp?]
At what time does it close?	**Hoe laat sluit hy?** [hu lãt slœit haj?]
Is it far?	**Is dit ver?** [is dit fer?]
Can I get there on foot?	**Kan ek soontoe stap?** [kan ek soentu stap?]
Can you show me on the map?	**Kan u dit op die stadskaart aanwys?** [kan u dit op di statskãrt ãnwajs?]
Please give me something for ...	**Gee my iets vir ... asseblief** [χeə maj its fir ... asseblif]
a headache	**koppyn** [koppajn]
a cough	**hoes** [hus]
a cold	**verkoudheid** [ferkæʊdhæjt]
the flu	**griep** [χrip]
a fever	**koors** [koərs]
a stomach ache	**maagpyn** [mãχpajn]
nausea	**naarheid** [nãrhæjt]
diarrhea	**diarree** [diarreə]
constipation	**konstipasie** [koŋstipasi]
pain in the back	**rugpyn** [ruχpajn]

chest pain	**borspyn** [borspajn]
side stitch	**steek in my sy** [steek in maj saj]
abdominal pain	**pyn in my onderbuik** [pajn in maj ondərbœik]

pill	**pil** [pil]
ointment, cream	**salf, room** [salf, roəm]
syrup	**stroop** [stroəp]
spray	**sproeier** [sprujer]
drops	**druppels** [druppɛls]

You need to go to the hospital.	**U moet hospitaal toe gaan.** [u mut hospitāl tu χān.]
health insurance	**siekteversekering** [siktə·fersekeriŋ]
prescription	**voorskrif** [foərskrif]
insect repellant	**insekmiddel** [insek·middəl]
Band Aid	**kleefverband** [kleəffər·bant]

The bare minimum

Excuse me, ...	**Verskoon my, ...** [ferskoən maj, ...]
Hello.	**Hallo.** [hallo.]
Thank you.	**Baie dankie.** [baje danki.]
Good bye.	**Totsiens.** [totsiŋs.]
Yes.	**Ja.** [ja.]
No.	**Nee.** [neə.]
I don't know.	**Ek weet nie.** [ɛk veet ni.]
Where? | Where to? | When?	**Waar? | Waarheen? | Wanneer?** [vãr? | vãrheən? | vanneər?]
I need ...	**Ek het ... nodig** [ɛk het ... nodəχ]
I want ...	**Ek wil ...** [ɛk vil ...]
Do you have ...?	**Het u ...?** [het u ...?]
Is there a ... here?	**Is hier 'n ...?** [is hir ə ...?]
May I ...?	**Mag ek ...?** [maχ ek ...?]
..., please (polite request)	**... asseblief** [... asseblif]
I'm looking for ...	**Ek soek ...** [ɛk suk ...]
restroom	**toilet** [tojlet]
ATM	**OTM** [o·te·em]
pharmacy (drugstore)	**apteek** [apteək]
hospital	**hospitaal** [hospitãl]
police station	**polisiekantoor** [polisi·kantoər]
subway	**moltrein** [moltræjn]

taxi	**taxi** [taksi]
train station	**stasie** [stasi]

My name is ...	**My naam is ...** [maj nãm is ...]
What's your name?	**Wat is u naam?** [vat is u nãm?]
Could you please help me?	**Kan u my help, asseblief?** [kan u maj hɛlp, asseblif?]
I've got a problem.	**Ek het 'n probleem.** [ɛk het ə probleəm.]
I don't feel well.	**Ek voel nie lekker nie.** [ɛk ful ni lɛkkər ni.]
Call an ambulance!	**Bel 'n ambulans!** [bel ə ambulaŋs!]
May I make a call?	**Kan ek 'n oproep maak?** [kan ɛk ə oprup mãk?]

I'm sorry.	**Jammer.** [jammər.]
You're welcome.	**Plesier.** [plesir.]

I, me	**Ek, my** [ek, maj]
you (inform.)	**jy** [jaj]
he	**hy** [haj]
she	**sy** [saj]
they (masc.)	**hulle** [hullə]
they (fem.)	**hulle** [hullə]
we	**ons** [ɔŋs]
you (pl)	**julle** [jullə]
you (sg, form.)	**u** [u]

ENTRANCE	**INGANG** [inχaŋ]
EXIT	**UITGANG** [œitχaŋ]
OUT OF ORDER	**BUITE WERKING** [bœitə verkiŋ]
CLOSED	**GESLUIT** [χeslœit]

OPEN	**OOP** [oəp]
FOR WOMEN	**DAMES** [dames]
FOR MEN	**MANS** [maŋs]

MINI DICTIONARY

This section contains 250 useful words required for everyday communication. You will find the names of months and days of the week here. The dictionary also contains topics such as colors, measurements, family, and more

T&P Books Publishing

DICTIONARY CONTENTS

T&P Books Publishing

time	**tyd**	[tajt]
hour	**uur**	[ɪr]
half an hour	**n halfuur**	[n halfɪr]
minute	**minuut**	[minɪt]
second	**sekonde**	[sekondə]
today (adv)	**vandag**	[fandaχ]
tomorrow (adv)	**môre**	[morə]
yesterday (adv)	**gister**	[χistər]
Monday	**Maandag**	[mãndaχ]
Tuesday	**Dinsdag**	[dinsdaχ]
Wednesday	**Woensdag**	[voɛŋsdaχ]
Thursday	**Donderdag**	[dondərdaχ]
Friday	**Vrydag**	[frajdaχ]
Saturday	**Saterdag**	[satərdaχ]
Sunday	**Sondag**	[sondaχ]
day	**dag**	[daχ]
working day	**werksdag**	[verks·daχ]
public holiday	**openbare vakansiedag**	[openbarə fakaŋsi·daχ]
weekend	**naweek**	[naveək]
week	**week**	[veək]
last week (adv)	**laas week**	[lãs veək]
next week (adv)	**volgende week**	[folχendə veək]
in the morning	**soggens**	[soχɛŋs]
in the afternoon	**in die namiddag**	[in di namiddaχ]
in the evening	**saans**	[sãŋs]
tonight (this evening)	**vanaand**	[fanãnt]
at night	**snags**	[snaχs]
midnight	**middernag**	[middərnaχ]
January	**Januarie**	[januari]
February	**Februarie**	[februari]
March	**Maart**	[mãrt]
April	**April**	[april]
May	**Mei**	[mæj]
June	**Junie**	[juni]
July	**Julie**	[juli]
August	**Augustus**	[ɔuχustus]

September	September	[septembər]
October	Oktober	[oktobər]
November	November	[nofembər]
December	Desember	[desembər]

in spring	in die lente	[in di lentə]
in summer	in die somer	[in di somər]
in fall	in die herfs	[in di herfs]
in winter	in die winter	[in di vintər]

month	maand	[mãnt]
season (summer, etc.)	seisoen	[sæjsun]
year	jaar	[jãr]

2. Numbers. Numerals

0 zero	nul	[nul]
1 one	een	[eən]
2 two	twee	[tweə]
3 three	drie	[dri]
4 four	vier	[fir]

5 five	vyf	[fajf]
6 six	ses	[ses]
7 seven	sewe	[sevə]
8 eight	ag	[aχ]
9 nine	nege	[neχə]
10 ten	tien	[tin]

11 eleven	elf	[ɛlf]
12 twelve	twaalf	[twãlf]
13 thirteen	dertien	[dertin]
14 fourteen	veertien	[feərtin]
15 fifteen	vyftien	[fajftin]

16 sixteen	sestien	[sestin]
17 seventeen	sewetien	[sevətin]
18 eighteen	agtien	[aχtin]
19 nineteen	negetien	[neχetin]

20 twenty	twintig	[twintəχ]
30 thirty	dertig	[dertəχ]
40 forty	veertig	[feərtəχ]
50 fifty	vyftig	[fajftəχ]

60 sixty	sestig	[sestəχ]
70 seventy	sewentig	[seventəχ]
80 eighty	tagtig	[taχtəχ]
90 ninety	negentig	[neχentəχ]
100 one hundred	honderd	[hondərt]

200 two hundred	**tweehonderd**	[twee·hondərt]
300 three hundred	**driehonderd**	[dri·hondərt]
400 four hundred	**vierhonderd**	[fir·hondərt]
500 five hundred	**vyfhonderd**	[fajf·hondərt]
600 six hundred	**seshonderd**	[ses·hondərt]
700 seven hundred	**sewehonderd**	[sevə·hondərt]
800 eight hundred	**aghonderd**	[aχ·hondərt]
900 nine hundred	**negehonderd**	[neχə·hondərt]
1000 one thousand	**duisend**	[dœisent]
10000 ten thousand	**tienduisend**	[tin·dœisent]
one hundred thousand	**honderdduisend**	[hondərt·dajsent]
million	**miljoen**	[miljun]
billion	**miljard**	[miljart]

3. Humans. Family

man (adult male)	**man**	[man]
young man	**jongman**	[joŋman]
woman	**vrou**	[fræʊ]
girl (young woman)	**meisie**	[mæjsi]
old man	**ou man**	[æʊ man]
old woman	**ou vrou**	[æʊ fræʊ]
mother	**moeder**	[mudər]
father	**vader**	[fadər]
son	**seun**	[søən]
daughter	**dogter**	[doχtər]
brother	**broer**	[brur]
sister	**suster**	[sustər]
parents	**ouers**	[æʊers]
child	**kind**	[kint]
children	**kinders**	[kindərs]
stepmother	**stiefma**	[stifma]
stepfather	**stiefpa**	[stifpa]
grandmother	**ouma**	[æʊma]
grandfather	**oupa**	[æʊpa]
grandson	**kleinseun**	[klæjn·søən]
granddaughter	**kleindogter**	[klæjn·doχtər]
grandchildren	**kleinkinders**	[klæjn·kindərs]
uncle	**oom**	[oəm]
aunt	**tante**	[tantə]
nephew	**neef**	[neəf]
niece	**nig**	[niχ]
wife	**vrou**	[fræʊ]

husband	man	[man]
married (masc.)	getroud	[χetræʊt]
married (fem.)	getroud	[χetræʊt]
widow	weduwee	[veduveə]
widower	wedunaar	[vedunãr]

| name (first name) | voornaam | [foərnãm] |
| surname (last name) | van | [fan] |

relative	familielid	[famililit]
friend (masc.)	vriend	[frint]
friendship	vriendskap	[frindskap]

partner	maat	[mãt]
superior (n)	baas	[bãs]
colleague	kollega	[kolleχa]
neighbors	bure	[burə]

4. Human body

body	liggaam	[liχχãm]
heart	hart	[hart]
blood	bloed	[blut]
brain	brein	[bræjn]

bone	been	[beən]
spine (backbone)	ruggraat	[ruχ·χrãt]
rib	rib	[rip]
lungs	longe	[loŋə]
skin	vel	[fəl]

head	kop	[kop]
face	gesig	[χesəχ]
nose	neus	[nøəs]
forehead	voorhoof	[foərhoəf]
cheek	wang	[vaŋ]

mouth	mond	[mont]
tongue	tong	[toŋ]
tooth	tand	[tant]
lips	lippe	[lippə]
chin	ken	[ken]

ear	oor	[oər]
neck	nek	[nek]
eye	oog	[oəχ]
pupil	pupil	[pupil]
eyebrow	wenkbrou	[vɛnk·bræʊ]
eyelash	ooghaar	[oəχ·hãr]
hair	haar	[hãr]

hairstyle	kapsel	[kapsəl]
mustache	snor	[snor]
beard	baard	[bãrt]
to have (a beard, etc.)	dra	[dra]
bald (adj)	kaal	[kãl]

hand	hand	[hant]
arm	arm	[arm]
finger	vinger	[fiŋər]
nail	nael	[naəl]
palm	palm	[palm]

shoulder	skouer	[skæʋər]
leg	been	[beən]
knee	knie	[kni]
heel	hakskeen	[hak·skeən]
back	rug	[ruχ]

5. Clothing. Personal accessories

clothes	klere	[klerə]
coat (overcoat)	jas	[jas]
fur coat	pelsjas	[pelʃas]
jacket (e.g., leather ~)	baadjie	[bãdʒi]
raincoat (trenchcoat, etc.)	reënjas	[reɛnjas]

shirt (button shirt)	hemp	[hemp]
pants	broek	[bruk]
suit jacket	baadjie	[bãdʒi]
suit	pak	[pak]

dress (frock)	rok	[rok]
skirt	romp	[romp]
T-shirt	T-hemp	[te-hemp]
bathrobe	badjas	[batjas]
pajamas	pajama	[pajama]
workwear	werksklere	[verks·klerə]

underwear	onderklere	[ondərklerə]
socks	sokkies	[sokkis]
bra	bra	[bra]
pantyhose	kousbroek	[kæʋsbruk]
stockings (thigh highs)	kouse	[kæʋsə]
bathing suit	baaikostuum	[bãj·kostɪm]

hat	hoed	[hut]
footwear	skoeisel	[skuisəl]
boots (e.g., cowboy ~)	laarse	[lãrsə]
heel	hak	[hak]
shoestring	skoenveter	[skun·fetər]

shoe polish	skoenpolitoer	[skun·politur]
gloves	handskoene	[handskunə]
mittens	duimhandskoene	[dœim·handskunə]
scarf (muffler)	serp	[serp]
glasses (eyeglasses)	bril	[bril]
umbrella	sambreel	[sambreəl]

tie (necktie)	das	[das]
handkerchief	sakdoek	[sakduk]
comb	kam	[kam]
hairbrush	haarborsel	[hãr·borsəl]

buckle	gespe	[χespə]
belt	belt	[bɛlt]
purse	beursie	[bøərsi]

6. House. Apartment

apartment	woonstel	[voəŋstəl]
room	kamer	[kamər]
bedroom	slaapkamer	[slãp·kamər]
dining room	eetkamer	[eət·kamər]

living room	sitkamer	[sit·kamər]
study (home office)	studeerkamer	[studeər·kamər]
entry room	ingangsportaal	[inχaŋs·portãl]
bathroom (room with a bath or shower)	badkamer	[bad·kamər]
half bath	toilet	[tojlet]

vacuum cleaner	stofsuier	[stof·sœiər]
mop	mop	[mop]
dust cloth	stoflap	[stoflap]
short broom	kort besem	[kort besem]
dustpan	skoppie	[skoppi]

furniture	meubels	[møəbɛls]
table	tafel	[tafel]
chair	stoel	[stul]
armchair	gemakstoel	[χemak·stul]

mirror	spieël	[spiɛl]
carpet	mat	[mat]
fireplace	vuurherd	[fɪr·hert]
drapes	gordyne	[χordajnə]
table lamp	tafellamp	[tafel·lamp]
chandelier	kroonlugter	[kroən·luχtər]

| kitchen | kombuis | [kombœis] |
| gas stove (range) | gasstoof | [χas·stoəf] |

| electric stove | elektriese stoof | [elektrisə stoəf] |
| microwave oven | mikrogolfoond | [mikroχolf·oent] |

refrigerator	yskas	[ajs·kas]
freezer	vrieskas	[friskas]
dishwasher	skottelgoedwasser	[skottɛlχud·wassər]
faucet	kraan	[krãn]

meat grinder	vleismeul	[flæjs·møəl]
juicer	versapper	[fersappər]
toaster	broodrooster	[broəd·roəstər]
mixer	menger	[meŋər]

coffee machine	koffiemasjien	[koffi·maʃin]
kettle	fluitketel	[flœit·ketəl]
teapot	teepot	[teə·pot]

TV set	TV-stel	[te·fe-stəl]
VCR (video recorder)	videomasjien	[video·maʃin]
iron (e.g., steam ~)	strykyster	[strajk·ajstər]
telephone	telefoon	[telefoən]

www.ingramcontent.com/pod-product-compliance
Lightning Source LLC
Chambersburg PA
CBHW070837050426
42452CB00011B/2321